Written by JOHN SHANNON,
O.B.E., D.Univ. (York),
Chairman, York Civic Trust

Introduction

York, the second city in England, is unique in that within its walls it has a more complete cycle of English architecture than any other English city.

Founded by the Romans in AD 71, at the confluence of two rivers, the Ouse and the Foss, its choice as a northern bastion of the Roman Empire reflects the military prescience of the Romans and their eye for an important strategic position. It is one of the great walled cities of Europe, with its original medieval walls some 2¼ miles in extent still encircling it. Within those walls medieval man built the largest cathedral in England, a great Benedictine abbey, 40 parish churches (of which some 20 survive today) and 14 other religious foundations.

A major city of the Roman Empire – Constantine was here proclaimed emperor – York was in the days of Alcuin a great centre of learning and culture, but reached its zenith in the Middle Ages, of which period its finely preserved guildhalls and churches are a potent reminder.

During the time of its greatest prosperity it was a base for Parliament and the home of kings, and during the Civil War a major royalist stronghold, but with the passing years and its diminishing importance as a port it became something of a backwater. It revived in Georgian times when the nobility of the period saw it as a place in which to build their fine houses, and later in the Victorian era when the coming of the railways and its chocolate industry gave to it a sound economic base which it has never since lost.

And so it has emerged into the twentieth century relatively unscathed: a joy to live in and exciting and rewarding to visit.

York, qui est la deuxième ville d'Angleterre, est unique du fait qu'elle offre à l'intérieur de ses murs l'éventail le plus complet d'architecture anglaise. Certaines villes possèdent plus de vestiges romains, d'autres plus de constructions du 18e siècle ou de maisons à colombage, mais aucune n'offre une telle variété. Fondée en 71 après J.-C. au confluent des rivières Ouse et Foss, la ville fut choisie comme bastion nordique de l'empire romain, ce qui illustre bien la prescience militaire et le flair des romains.

York est l'une des plus importantes cités fortifiées d'Europe, encerclée par sa muraille médiévale, de près de 4 kilomètres de long, qui semble la protéger contre les dégâts du progrès comme elle l'a protégée contre les envahisseurs dans le passé. Entre ces murs fut construite au moyen-âge la plus grande cathédrale d'Angleterre, une grande abbaye bénédictine, 40 églises paroissiales (dont 20 ont survécu jusqu'à nos jours) et 14 autres édifices religieux. Toutes ces constructions s'établirent sur le tracé des rues romaines, encore visible de nos jours. Les noms des rues témoignent de l'influence viking.

Ville d'importance majeure sous l'empire romain – c'est là que Constantin fut proclamé empereur – York était, au temps d'Alcuin, un grand centre culturel, mais elle atteint son zénith au moyen-âge, dont la présence nous est rappelée par ses églises et hôtels finement préservés.

Au temps de sa grande prospérité, York fut le siège du parlement et la résidence des rois et pendant la guerre civile une place forte du royalisme. La fin du moyen-âge vit son plus grand développement architectural mais au fil des ans l'importance de York en tant que port diminua, et elle arriva à une certaine stagnation. C'est au 18e siècle qu'elle connut une renaissance quand la noblesse de l'époque y construit ses belles demeures, et plus tard à l'époque victorienne quand l'avènement des chemins de fer et de l'industrie du chocolat lui donnèrent une solide base économique qu'elle a toujours gardée depuis.

C'est ainsi que York est parvenue au 20e siècle relativement intacte, faisant la joie de ses habitants et de ses visiteurs.

York, die zweite Stadt in England, ist einzigartig dadurch, daß sie in ihren Mauern ein größeres Spektrum an englischen Baustilen besitzt als jede andere englische Stadt.

Im Jahre 71 von den Römern gegründet, reflektiert die Lage dieses nördlichen Bollwerks des römischen Reiches am Zusammenfluß der beiden Flüsse Ouse und Foss die militärische Umsicht der Römer und ihr Gespür für eine günstige strategische Position.

York ist eine der großen von Mauern umgebenen Städte in Europa. Die originalen mittelalterlichen Wälle erstrecken sich über eine Länge von 3½ Kilometern und scheinen die Stadt heute vor den schlimmsten Auswüchsen des modernen Fortschritts zu schützen, wie sie sie einst vor Angreifern schützten. Innerhalb dieser Mauern baute man im Mittelalter die größte Kathedrale in England, eine große Benediktinerabtei, 40 Gemeindekirchen (von denen 20 bis heute überlebt haben) und 14 andere kirchliche Gründungen.

Schon während der römischen Ära eine bedeutende Stadt (Konstantin wurde hier zum Kaiser ausgerufen), wurde York zu Alkuins Zeiten ein wichtiges Zentrum für Gelehrsamkeit und Kultur, erreichte aber seinen Höhepunkt im Mittelalter, woran die sorgsam erhaltenen Gildehäuser und Kirchen erinnern.

Während der Zeit seiner größten Wohlhabenheit war York Sitz des Parlaments und verschiedener Könige und während des Bürgerkrieges ein wichtiger königlicher Stützpunkt. Im späten Mittelalter genoß die Stadt ihre höchste bauliche Entwicklung, fiel aber aufgrund der schwindenden Bedeutung als Handelshafen allmählich in einen Dornröschenschlaf, aus dem sie erst zu georgischen Zeiten erwachte, als die damaligen Adligen York als Sitz für ihre feinen Häuser erkoren. Eine weitere Belebung erfuhr die Stadt in der viktorianischen Ära durch die Eisenbahn und die Schokoladenindustrie, die ihr heute noch eine gesunde wirtschaftliche Basis geben.

The Defences

The city walls and Clifford's Tower are today the main visible reminders of the military importance of the city in medieval and earlier times. The walls extend in length for some 2¼ miles, and except for one stretch where the presence of marshy ground made such defence unnecessary, surround the whole city. They are punctuated at intervals by the four great gateways to the city: Micklegate Bar, Monk Bar, Walmgate Bar and Bootham Bar, only one of which (Walmgate Bar)

retains its barbican.

The Castle of York – Clifford's Tower – stands on a motte, or mound, built by William the Conqueror which, with a similar motte on the far side of the river, guarded the approach to the city from this direction. The present Clifford's Tower was built in the thirteenth century, its quatrefoil plan being unique in England, although one exists at Etampes in France. A wooden castle rebuilt by the Conqueror was the scene of a massacre of the Jews in 1190 during the reign of Richard I. The thirteenth-century castle was reduced to its present state in the seventeenth century after its powder magazine had exploded.

Micklegate Bar, the gateway to London and the south.

◄ Clifford's Tower from an eighteenth-century print, showing its dominant position.

The city walls, looking towards Monk Bar. They form an elevated sidewalk from which the medieval city can be viewed.

Walmgate Bar; by J. Mulholland.

Le mur d'enceinte s'étend sur près de 4 kilomètres, ponctué par quatre grandes portes d'accès à la ville : Micklegate Bar, Monk Bar, Walmgate Bar et Bootham Bar. Walmgate Bar est la seule qui possède encore sa tour de garde.

Le château de York – Clifford's Tower – se dresse sur une butte érigée par Guillaume le Conquérant qui en fit aménager une semblable de l'autre côté de la rivière, défendant ainsi l'approche de la ville dans cette direction. La tour actuelle fut construite au 13ᵉ siècle sur un plan en quatre-feuilles unique en Angleterre (on en trouve un semblable à Etampes). Le château du 13ᵉ siècle fut réduit à son état actuel par l'explosion de sa poudrière au 17ᵉ siècle.

Die Stadtmauer erstreckt sich über eine Länge von 3½ Kilometern und wird in Abständen durch vier große Tore unterbrochen: Micklegate Bar, Monk Bar, Walmgate Bar und Bootham Bar. Nur Walmgate Bar ist noch als Tor vorhanden.

Die Burg von York, Clifford's Tower, steht auf einem von Wilhelm dem Eroberer errichteten Erdhügel und beherrschte mit einem ähnlichen Hügel auf der anderen Seite des Flusses den Zugang zur Stadt aus dieser Richtung. Der Turm wurde im 13. Jahrhundert gebaut, sein kleeblattförmiger Grundriß ist einzigartig in England (es gibt einen weiteren in Etampes in Frankreich). Die Burg wurde im 17. Jahrhundert durch eine Explosion des Pulvermagazins schwer beschädigt.

Monk Bar; from an old print by J. Mulholland. ►

Above: **Bootham Bar and Minster at night.** *Centre:* **The City Wall.**
Below: **Micklegate Bar, the great gateway to the south and the traditional entry point for the sovereigns of England.**

The Minster from the north; by Albert Goodwin, 1904.

Above: Monk Bar from the city walls.
Centre: The city wall walkway.
Below: Walmgate Bar from its barbican – the only one to remain, the others having been demolished in the eighteenth and nineteenth centuries.

York Minster

▲ **The Minster with St Michael-le-Belfrey.**

York Minster (the name derives from the word *monasterium* though it was never a monastery; it means a teaching settlement) is not only England's biggest cathedral, it is indeed the biggest medieval building of any kind in the country. It is one of the finest examples of Gothic architecture, the building of which commenced in 1220 and finished in 1472. The full cycle of English architecture is represented in this one building, and nearly half of England's medieval stained glass fills its 126 windows. It dominates the city today, and must certainly have done so in medieval times, its central tower being 198 feet high and its two western towers 196 feet high.

It was entirely restored between 1967 and 1972 at a cost of £2,000,000. The restoration was completed by washing down the whole of the inside and outside of the building, so that it can be seen today as it must have appeared to medieval eyes.

York Minster est la plus grande cathédrale d'Angleterre. Elle représente l'un des plus beaux exemples d'architecture gothique. Sa construction commença en 1220 et se termina en 1472. La tour centrale est haute de 61 mètres et les deux tours occidentales sont hautes de 60 mètres. Ses 126 ouvertures contiennent presque la moitié des vitraux médiévaux d'Angleterre.

La cathédrale fut entièrement restaurée entre 1967 et 1972, pour une somme de 2 millions de livres.

Das Münster von York ist die größte Kirche von England. Es ist eines der schönsten Beispiele für gotische Architektur und wurde 1220 begonnen und 1472 vollendet. Der Mittelturm ist 61 Meter und die beiden westlichen Türme 60 Meter hoch. Die 126 Fenster enthalten fast die Hälfte der noch erhaltenen mittelalterlichen Glasmalerei in England.

The Minster from the east. ▶

The west front.

The Minster from the north east.

◄ The great east window.

The great east window of the Minster – the largest expanse of stained glass in England – was made between 1405 and 1408 by John Thornton of Coventry. 'God Enthroned' is at the apex of the window, with Old Testament figures below and twenty-seven panels portraying scenes from Genesis and Revelation.

The Chapter House was built *c.* 1260 to 1265. A noteworthy feature of it is that it has no central pillar. Near the entrance are painted on the wall in Latin the words: 'As the rose is the flower of flowers, so this is the building of buildings'. The roof bosses are medieval. The stained glass in its seven windows is particularly fine, and they were originally glazed in 1300 to 1307. The stone carvings are worthy of note.

The South Transept roof, destroyed by fire in 1984 has, with its great Rose Window, been superbly restored. Amongst the new bosses are those designed by children for the BBC's *Blue Peter* programme.

Le grand vitrail est de la cathédrale fut exécuté de 1405 à 1408 par John Thornton de Coventry.

La salle du chapitre fut construite de 1260 à 1265 environ. Un des points les plus remarquables à noter est l'absence de pilier central.

Comble du transept sud, restauré avec sa superbe rosace après sa destruction par le feu en 1984. Parmi les clefs du voûte, noter celles conçues par des enfants pour l'émission de la BBC *Blue Peter*.

Das große Ostfenster des Münsters, die größte Fläche an bemaltem Glas in England, wurde zwischen 1405 und 1408 von John Thornton aus Coventry geschaffen.

Das Chapter House wurde zwischen 1260 und 1265 erbaut. Es ist bemerkenswert durch das Fehlen eines zentralen Stützpfeilers.

Das Dach des Südquerschiffes wurde 1984 durch Feuer zerstört. Das große Rosettenfenster ist prächtig restauriert worden. Einige der neuen Bossen haben Kinder für das BBC Programm «Blauer Peter» entworfen.

Stone carving in the Chapter House.
Inset: **The Rose Window.** ►

Art & Culture York's Museums

York's museums are among the finest in the country. The oldest of them is the Yorkshire Museum in the Museum Gardens, established by the Yorkshire Philosophical Society in 1827 and containing a very fine Roman and Natural History collection. The gardens themselves (laid out by the Society) are noteworthy for their fine collection of trees.

The National Railway Museum, with its fine collection of railway engines, rolling stock and memorabilia, has proved to be one of the most visited museums in England. But it is at the other side of the city, in the area of Clifford's Tower that the cultural life of the city has been dramatically enhanced. For within a stone's throw of each other are the Castle Museum, without doubt the finest folk museum in the country; the York Story, told by means of models, murals and audio-visual techniques in an imaginative and exciting manner within the fine redundant medieval church of St Mary, Castlegate; and the Viking Centre, with its dramatic and evocative reconstruction of the York viking settlement Jorvik, set below ground on the very soil on which the original viking houses were discovered. The Bar Convent Museum

of Christianity is in Blossom Street – the glazed entrance hall and the neo-classical chapel are alone worth the visit. Finally, there is the latest contribution to York's cultural wealth – Fairfax House (1762) said to be the finest Georgian townhouse in England, beautifully restored by the York Civic Trust at a cost of £¾m. and containing a collection of Georgian furniture and clocks valued by Christie's at over £2m.

Les musées de York comptent parmi les meilleurs du pays; son plus ancien, le Yorkshire Museum (1827) est entouré d'admirables jardins.

C'est à York que l'on trouve le musée anglais des chemins de fer (National Railway Museum), l'un des plus visités d'Angleterre. De l'autre côté de la ville, près de Clifford's Tower, se trouvent le Castle Museum (musée des arts et traditions populaires), l'église St-Mary où l'on donne un spectacle sur la ville, « The York Story », et le Viking Centre où est reconstitué Jorvik, le camp viking de York. Musée de la chrétienté de Bar Convent dans Blossom Street – le hall vitré d'entrée et la chapelle néo-classique en justifient la visite. Enfin, Fairfax House (1762), considérée comme l'une des plus magnifiques résidences de style anglais classique (georgien) du pays, vient d'être superbement restaurée. On admirera les moulures et boiseries et la collec-

tion de meubles et horloges.
Yorks Museen zählen zu den besten im Lande. Das älteste ist das Yorkshire Museum in den Museumsgärten und von der Yorkshire Philosophischen Gesellschaft 1827 gegründet. Die Gärten sind berühmt für ihren prächtigen Baumbestand.

Das nationale Eisenbahnmuseum beherbergt u. a. eine stattliche Lokomotivensammlung. Am anderen Ende der Stadt um den Clifford Turm liegen nahe beieinander das Burgmuseum, eines der besten Volksmuseen des Landes; die mittelalterliche Kirche St. Mary in Castlegate, in der Yorks Geschichte mittels Modellen, Wandgemälden und Filmvorführungen geschildert wird und das Wikingerzentrum, wo man die alte Wikingersiedlung Jorvic rekonstruiert hat. Das Bar Convent Museum des Christentums befindet sich in Blossom Street – sein schön verglaster Eingang und die klassizistische Kapelle sind allein schön einen Besuch wert. Das Fairfax Haus (1762) gilt als eines der schönsten, georgianischen Stadthäuser. Vom York Civic Trust wundervoll restauriert beherbergt es eine Sammlung georgianischer Möbel und Uhren, die von Christie auf über zwei Millionen Pfund geschätzt worden ist.

Opposite: **Fairfax House, Castlegate** *by courtesy of the York Civic Trust.*

Below: **A viking street** *by courtesy of the Jorvik Viking Centre*

Some Minor Pleasures of York

A fire mark.

Yorkshire Museum.

Medieval painted glass in York Minster.

The York Story – St Mary's Church.

The York Story – model of the Shambles.

The York Story – the St James Window.

The Bar Convent Museum of Christianity.

The Castle Museum.

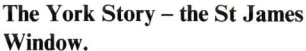

William Etty & The Art Gallery

The City Art Gallery, a building of Italianate style in Exhibition Square, houses one of the best provincial art collections in the country. It contains many old masters, notably the Lycett Green collection, and some excellent examples of early twentieth-century English paintings, including ones by Sickert, Steer, and Whistler. There are in addition prints, early drawings, and photographs of the city.

In front of the Art Gallery stands the statue of William Etty, R.A. (1787–1849), who is perhaps best known for his painting of the nude figure, and the Art Gallery contains many of his works. But not only was he an artist of repute: he was the conservationist of his era, and played a leading part in helping to preserve the old city from the march of Victorian 'progress'. He was largely responsible for the preservation of the city walls, and at the foot of his statue there is a model of Bootham Bar, to which he looks and which he was responsible for saving.

La galerie d'art de la ville contient l'une des meilleures collections d'art de province. Elle contient de nombreuses œuvres de peintres classiques et des tableaux de Sickert, Steer et Whistler.

En face de la galerie se dresse la statue de William Etty, R.A. (1787–1849), célèbre surtout pour ses portraits de nus (on trouve un grand nombre de ses œuvres dans la galerie).

Il ne se contenta pas d'être un artiste renommé, mais joua un rôle majeur dans la protection de la ville contre les « progrès » de l'époque victorienne.

Art Gallery and Etty statue.

Die Städtische Kunstgallerie beherbergt eine der besten Kunstsammlungen der englischen Provinz. Sie enthält Alte Meister und Gemälde von Sickert, Steer und Whistler.

Vor der Kunstgallerie steht die Statue von William Etty, R.A. (1787–1849), der wohl am besten bekannt ist durch seine Aktmalerei; die Gallerie besitzt viele seiner Werke. Aber er war nicht nur ein berühmter Künstler, sondern auch ein Denkmalsschützer seiner Zeit, und er spielte eine führende Rolle bei der Bewahrung der alten Stadt vor dem viktorianischen „Fortschritt".

Venus and Cupid (*c*. 1830); by William Etty, R.A.

Monk Bar; by William Etty, R.A.

A York Panorama

Although York may be said to have reached the zenith of its historical influence in the Middle Ages, the best was yet to come. Romantic though the medieval era sounds, it was in fact a time of smell and disease. York had developed as a thriving medieval township which ranked with London, Norwich and Bristol in commercial and political importance. It was during this era that it has been described as 'a city of exquisite architecture rising out of a midden'.

As Hull took over as a port and the city's influence on national affairs diminished, it became a stagnant backwater and was to remain as such until it was touched by the wealth of Georgian gentry and later still by the coming of the railways and its rebirth as a centre of communications. By-passed by the Industrial Revolution (which, encouraged by the presence of coal, erupted largely in the West Riding), its very unimportance during those critical years was in fact to prove its salvation: most of its architectural treasures thereby survived the onward march of so-called progress which marred bigger cities of the kingdom. And neither the coming of the railways nor the establishment of its great chocolate industries by Rowntree and Terry militated against the architectural treasure-house which the city had, over the centuries, become. Indeed, the Georgian era brought to it a wealth of town-house architecture of the very highest order.

York was also fortunate in that the air raids of the Second World War did minimal damage to the historic core, and in that the craze for the commercial redevelopment of city centres in the 1960s largely passed it by. Thus, by the hand of God and man, has the city emerged largely unblemished.

York devint une ville florissante au moyen-âge, rivalisant avec Londres, Norwich et Bristol au point de vue commercial et politique.

Elle fut laissée de côté par la révolution industrielle (qui eut lieu principalement dans la région de West Riding en raison de la présence de charbon), et fut épargnée du fait de ce manque d'importance : la plupart de ses trésors architecturaux ont ainsi survécu à la marche du progrès. De plus, ni l'arrivée du chemin de fer, ni l'établissement de l'industrie du chocolat par Rowntree et Terry n'eurent d'influence néfaste sur les trésors d'architecture que la ville avait alors accumulés. En fait le 18e siècle et le début du 19e siècle y virent la construction de résidences urbaines de premier ordre.

Les raids aériens de la deuxième guerre mondiale firent peu de dégâts dans le centre historique et la grande vogue de modernisation des centres-villes des années 60 l'a épargné dans une très grand mesure. Ainsi, grâce à la nature et aux hommes, la ville d'York est parvenue au 20e siècle en grande partie intacte.

York entwickelte sich im Mittelalter zu einer blühenden Stadt, die sich in wirtschaftlicher und politischer Hinsicht mit London, Norwich und Bristol messen konnte.

Die industrielle Revolution, nahm keine Notiz von York. Dieser Umstand erwies sich als ein Segen; die meisten seiner baulichen Kostbarkeiten überlebten so den Vormarsch des sogenannten Fortschritts. Weder das Aufkommen der Eisenbahn noch die Gründung der großen Schokoladenfabriken von Rowntree und Terry erwiesen sich als Nachteile für die architektonische Schatzkammer, zu der sich die Stadt im Laufe der Jahrhunderte entwickelt hatte. In der Tat, die georgische Ära bescherte ihr einen Reichtum an städtischer Architektur.

York wurde in den Bombenangriffen des zweiten Weltkrieges in seinem historischen Kern glücklicherweise nur wenig beschädigt, und auch die Manie für kommerzielle Entwicklung der Cityzentren in den sechziger Jahren verschonte die Stadt.

Bird's-eye view of York in early Victorian times.

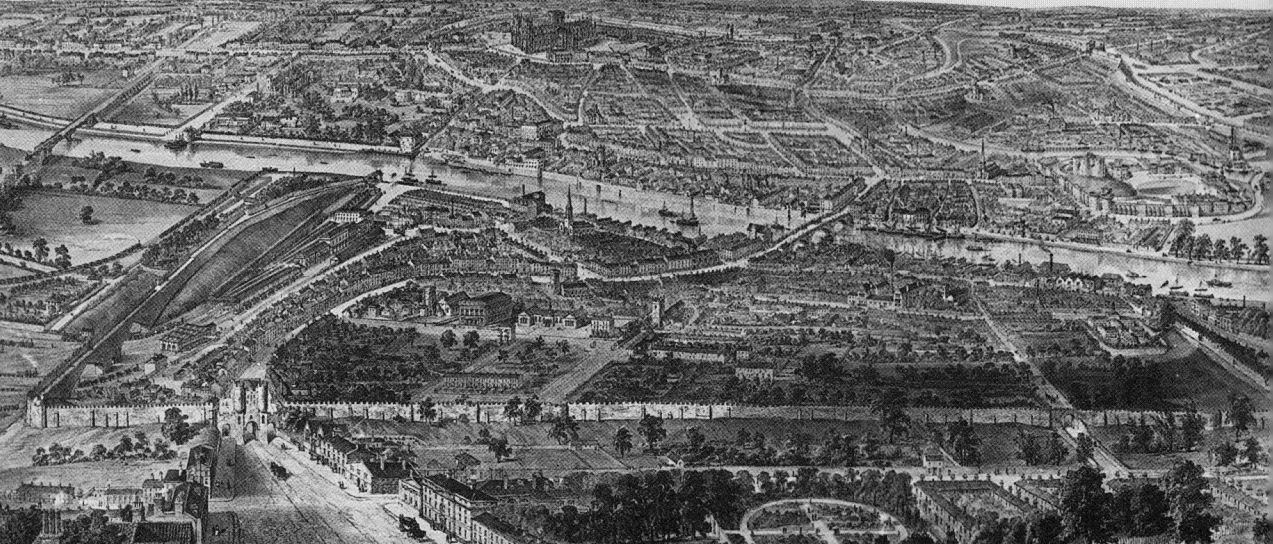

The Rivers of York

The two York rivers, the Ouse and the Foss, at the confluence of which the Romans established the city, have throughout the centuries played a major role in its commercial and cultural development. From its earliest days it was a thriving port, and in the Middle Ages the Merchant Adventurers' Company of York exercised, by their use of the Ouse, a potent influence upon the trade of the city and its hinterland, bringing commerce with the northern ports of Europe.

With the growth of Hull as a port, the importance of York diminished, but King's and Queen's Staiths are still evocative reminders of the city's mercantile greatness.

Nor has the value of the river as an amenity been neglected, and in 1730 the Corporation, in what must have been one of the first exercises in England in creating an environmental amenity, built the New Walk, described in its day as 'a noble promenade'.

The New Walk, from an eighteenth-century print.

Les deux rivières d'York, l'Ouse et la Foss, au confluent desquelles les romains établirent la ville, ont joué un rôle majeur au cours des siècles dans son développement commercial et culturel.

La valeur de ces rivières en tant qu'aménité n'a pas été négligée non plus et en 1730 la Corporation fit construire la Nouvelle Promenade (the New Walk), qui fut certainement l'un des premiers aménagements de l'environnement en Angleterre.

Die beiden Yorker Flüsse, Ouse und Foss, an deren Zusammenfluß die Römer die Stadt gründeten, spielten jahrhundertelang eine wichtige Rolle in ihrer wirtschaftlichen und kulturellen Entwicklung. Denn York war von Anfang an ein wichtiger Handelshafen.

Auch ist der Erholungswert des Flusses nicht unerkannt geblieben: 1730 ließ der Magistrat in einem der ersten Versuche in England, eine Erholungseinrichtung zu schaffen, den New Walk anlegen, seinerzeit als „eine elegante Promenade" beschrieben.

Old Ouse Bridge.

The Streets of York

The streets of York follow the medieval pattern superimposed on the roads of the Roman legionary fortress, with the occasional exception such as the late Regency crescent known as St Leonard's Place. Many of the street names bear witness to the Viking influence on the city's history, ending as they do in the word *gate* (being Scandinavian for a road or way). One street, Stonegate, has been a highway for 1,900 years.

Les rues d'York suivent le tracé des rues du moyen-âge qui elles-mêmes s'étaient superposées à celles de la forteresse de la légion romaine, avec quelques exceptions telles que la rue en arc de cercle de l'époque Régence connue sous le nom de St Leonard's Place.

De nombreux noms de rues témoignent de l'influence viking, car ils se terminent par le mot « gate » (« rue » en scandinave). L'une d'elles, Stonegate, existe depuis 1.900 ans.

Die Straßen von York folgen dem mittelalterlichen Stadtplan, der wiederum auf den Plan der römischen Legionärsfestung gebaut ist, mit gelegentlichen Ausnahmen wie dem Regency-Bogen St. Leonards's Place. Viele Straßennamen, die das skandinavische Wort „gate" zur Endung haben, bezeugen den wikingischen Einfluß auf die Geschicke der Stadt. Stonegate ist eine Straße seit 1900 Jahren.

St Leonard's Place.

The city escaped the worst features of the 'city-centre redevelopment' mania of the 1960s, and consequently the streets and their buildings are on a human scale. Behind many of the Georgian and Victorian façades there still exist the timber frames of the medieval properties, and a fascinating feature of many streets is the jettied buildings projecting over the pavement. The best and oldest example is Our Lady's Row in Goodramgate, while Stonegate, Petergate and the Shambles are unsurpassed in England.

The architectural development of the city can best be seen above the level of the shop fascias, and the streets are rich with minor architectural or historical delights, viz. **(1)** the Red Indian sign of a tobacconist in Petergate; the Little Admiral **(2)** over the clock **(3)** outside St Martin's in Coney Street; the chained red devil **(4)** in Stonegate; the torch extinguisher in Duncombe Place **(5)**; and the fire marks **(6)** in many of the historic streets.

On voit partout des exemples du développement architectural d'York. Les rues sont pleines de petits détails architecturaux ou historiques qui font les délices des voyageurs, **(1)** l'enseigne indienne d'un bureau de tabac dans Petergate ; le Petit Amiral **(2)** au-dessus de l'horloge **(3)** à l'extérieur de l'eglise Saint Martin dans Coney Street ; le diable rouge enchaîné **(4)** dans Stonegate ; l'extincteur de lampes dans Duncombe Place **(5)** ; et les plaques d'incendie **(6)** dans la plupart des rues historiques.

Die bauliche Entwicklung der Stadt läßt sich am besten oberhalb der Ladenfronten ablesen, und die Straßen sind reich an kleinen baulichen und historischen Köstlichkeiten, z. B. **(1)** der Indianer eines Tabakladens in Petergate; der kleine Admiral **(2)** über der Uhr **(3)** vor St. Martin's in Coney Street; der angekettete rote Teufel **(4)** in Stonegate; der Fackelauslöscher in Duncombe Place **(5)**; die Feuerversicherungsmarken **(6)** in vielen der alten Straßen.

Stonegate.

Three of York's most historic streets are The Shambles, High and Low Petergate, and Stonegate. The Shambles, a street which is a thousand years old, is the only York street to be mentioned in Domesday Book. Its name derives from the Anglo-Saxon word *shamel*, meaning a stall or bench, on which meat was displayed for sale, and for centuries it was the street of the butchers of York; indeed, until the mid twentieth century it still contained many butchers' shops. Its great number of medieval buildings, overhanging as they do the narrow road beneath, makes it unique among York streets.

Petergate, lying on the line of the Roman road from north-west to south-east and named after St Peter, the patron saint of the Minster, has a wealth of medieval, Victorian and Georgian buildings. A particularly attractive view of Petergate can be obtained from King's Square looking back towards the Minster.

Stonegate, which runs from St Helen's Square almost to the south door of the Minster, is perhaps the finest street in York. It contains the architecture of almost every age from Norman to Victorian times. A highway for almost 1,900 years, it probably derives its name from the fact that it was paved in Roman times and not from its being the street along which all of the stone for the Minster came from the river. It contains a great deal of interest, not least in that it was in this street that the parents of Guy Fawkes lived, he being baptised in the near-by church of St Michael-le-Belfrey.

Les rues les plus historiques d'York sont The Shambles, High Petergate et Low Petergate, et Stonegate. The Shambles a mille ans d'âge et est la seule rue mentionnée dans le grand cadastre d'Angleterre (Domesday Book). Ce qui la rend unique dans York c'est le grand nombre de maisons du moyen-âge surplombant la rue étroite.

Le nom de Petergate vient de Saint Pierre. Cette rue est très riche en constructions du moyen-âge, du 18e siècle et de l'époque victorienne ; on en obtient la meilleure vue en

Petergate.

Minster Gates. ▶

regardant de King's Square vers l'ouest.

Stonegate existe depuis près de 1.900 ans. C'est une rue pleine d'intérêt, par exemple les parents de Guy Fawkes y habitèrent et celui-ci fut baptisé dans l'église de Saint Michel-le-Belfrey toute proche.

Drei der ältesten Straßen in York sind The Shambles, High und Low Petergate und Stonegate. Die tausend Jahre alte Shambles ist die einzige Yorker Straße, die im Domesday Book erwähnt ist. Diese Straße mit ihren vielen überhängenden mittelalterlichen Häusern ist einzigartig unter den Straßen Yorks.

Petergate ist nach St. Peter benannt. Sie hat eine Vielzahl von mittelalterlichen, viktorianischen und georgischen Gebäuden. Einen besonders schönen Ausblick auf die Straße bekommt man vom King's Square aus zum Münster hin.

Stonegate ist wohl die schönste Straße in York und hat Bauwerke fast jeden Alters von der normannischen bis zur viktorianischen Zeit. Dies ist eine Straße gewesen seit fast 1900 Jahren. Hier lebten die Eltern von Guy Fawkes.

The Shambles.

The Historic Buildings of York

For the reasons given earlier in this book, a tremendous number of buildings of great historic and architectural quality have survived to the present day, and York contains no fewer than 960 buildings listed by the Government as being of historical or architectural importance. They are of every age, including, off Stonegate, the remains of the oldest house in York *in situ* – a Norman house.

They also include the great guildhalls (the Guildhall itself, the Merchant Adventurers' Hall, the Merchant Taylors' Hall and St Anthony's Hall) of the medieval period; the King's Manor (in which many kings of England have stayed and which was the headquarters of the Council of the North from *c.* 1540 to 1641); the great Minster itself (the largest cathedral north of

the Rhine); behind it the Treasurer's House, formerly the home of the Treasurer of the Minster and nowadays an amalgam of several ages of architecture; and some twenty medieval parish churches (out of an original total of forty), of which Holy Trinity, Goodramgate, is one of the most attractive.

Thanks largely to a community which over the centuries has cared for its inheritance, most of the buildings are in a very good state of preservation, and with the changed climate of public opinion in regard to the conservation of historic cities, their future is now assured. They provide a unique 'backdrop' to a study of the history of England and a practical workshop in which can be examined the problems of conserving the world's historic architecture.

In this connection the Institute of Advanced Architectural Studies (based in the King's Manor), part of the University of York, runs regular courses in conservation to which are attracted architects from all over the world.

Another reason why the lesser buildings of York within the historic core are so well preserved is the

operation by the City Council of what is called a Town Scheme, whereby any owner of a building requiring repair or restoration can obtain a grant of up to 50 per cent of the cost.

A further safeguard is that the whole of the historic core of the city is within a Conservation Area, which

---

Pour les raisons mentionnées plus haut, un très grand nombre de constructions du plus haut intérêt historique et architectural ont survécu jusqu'à nos jours et York ne possède pas moins de 960 bâtiments recensés par le gouvernement comme étant d'importance historique et architecturale. Ces constructions sont de toutes les époques et on trouve près de Stonegate la plus vieille maison d'York, de l'époque romane.

On trouve à York les anciens hôtels prestigieux du moyen-âge : l'Hôtel de Ville (Guildhall), l'hôtel des marchands aventuriers (Merchant Adventurers' Hall), l'hôtel des maîtres tailleurs (Merchant Taylors' Hall) et l'hôtel de Saint Antoine (St Anthony's Hall), ainsi que le Manoir

The Hospitium, Museum Gardens.

du Roi (King's Manor) dans lequel de nombreux rois d'Angleterre ont résidé et qui fut le siège du Conseil du Nord de 1540 à 1641 environ. On y trouve aussi la cathédrale (la plus grande au nord du Rhin) avec derrière la maison où résidait le trésorier de la cathédrale (Treasurer's House) et qui présente de nos jours un mélange de plusieurs styles d'architecture. N'oublions pas près de 20 églises paroissiales médiévales (il y en avait 40 à l'origine), dont l'église de la Sainte Trinité (Holy Trinity) dans Goodramgate est la plus jolie.

La plupart de ces bâtiments sont très bien préservés.

In York stehen nicht weniger als 960 Gebäude unter Denkmalsschutz. Sie haben jedes Alter, die Überreste des ältesten Hauses in York, nahe Stonegate, stammen von einem normannischen Haus.

Zu dieser Anzahl gehören die großen Gildehäuser des Mittelalters (die Guildhall selbst, die Merchant Adventurers' Hall, die Merchant Taylors' Hall und St. Anthony's Hall); die King's Manor; das große Münster selbst (die größte Kathedrale nördlich des Rheins); dahinter das Treasurer's House, einst die Residenz des Schatzmeisters des Münsters und heute ein Gemisch von verschiedenen Architekturen; und schließlich 20 mittelalterliche Gemeindekirchen (ursprünglich gab es 40), von denen Holy Trinity in Goodramgate eine der schönsten ist.

Above: **Treasurer's House.**
Centre: **The King's Manor.**
Below: **Holy Trinity, Goodramgate.**

St William's College.

gives the Local Authority wide powers of protection.

St William's College (*top*) is one of the best preserved timbered buildings in England. It was established in 1461 by Letters Patent granted to Warwick the Kingmaker as a college to house the Chantry Priests of the Minster. During the Civil War Charles I set up his printing-press here. The College, which has survived a chequered history largely intact, is open to the public. Visitors should note the attractive courtyard and the fine medieval wood-carvings on the side of the building.

Another fine example of a medieval town-house is the Thomas Herbert House in the Pavement. The Herberts were a very old York family, and one of them, Sir Thomas Herbert, became a great friend of Charles I, slept with him on the night

before his execution in Whitehall, and accompanied him on to the scaffold.

Among the old churches, All Saints', Pavement, is noteworthy for its fine belfry, in which for many years there hung a lantern set up to guide travellers across the then nearby Forest of Galtres. It has a fine thirteenth-century knocker on the north door.

Clifford's Tower, to which we have referred previously, stands near the Assize Courts, which were built, as was the Castle Museum opposite, by the famous York architect John Carr.

Le collège de Saint Guillaume (St William's College) (*en haut*) : pendant la guerre civile Charles Ier y installa son imprimerie. Il est maintenant ouvert au public.

Thomas Herbert House est un autre exemple d'architecture urbaine du moyen-âge.

L'église de la Toussaint est remarquable pour son beffroi.

Clifford's Tower fut construite au 13e siècle.

St. William's College (*oben*): Während des Bürgerkrieges stellte Charles I hier seine Druckpresse auf. Das College wird heute als öffentlicher Versammlungssaal benutzt.

Ein anderes gutes Beispiel für ein mittelalterliches Stadthaus ist das Thomas Herbert House im Pavement. All Saints', Pavement, ist bemerkenswert wegen seines schönen Glockenturms. Clifford's Tower wurde im 13. Jahrhundert auf einem von Wilhelm dem Eroberer aufgeworfenen Erdhügel erbaut.

Clifford's Tower. ▶

Our Lady's Row (*below*) in Goodramgate is noteworthy in that the houses, which are jettied (the overhangs being of *c.* 1320), are among the earliest of their type in England. They were built on the churchyard of Holy Trinity Church, which lies behind them, in order that the rents could pay for Masses to be said in the church. This church, to which reference is made elsewhere, is one of the finest in York, sitting in its own secluded and little-changed churchyard.

Cette rangée de maisons, bâties vers 1320 (Our Lady's Row, *ci-dessus*), dans Goodramgate est remarquable car elles sont parmi les plus anciennes maisons de ce type en Angleterre.

Our Lady's Row (*oben*) in Goodramgate ist bemerkenswert durch die Tatsache, daß die überhängenden Häuser zu den frühesten ihrer Art in England gehören (ca. 1320). Sie wurden auf dem Friedhof von Holy Trinity erbaut.

In the Shambles (*below*), from time immemorial the butchers' street, one can get the greatest atmosphere of a medieval street in York.

There are several possible reasons for buildings being jettied (i.e. having overhanging upper storeys). It may have been a means of getting more floor space in days when building land was very scarce; it may have been to protect the ground floor or to shelter a shop beneath; or it may have been a way of counteracting movement of the upper floors.

The Shambles (*ci-dessus*) fut de tout temps la rue des bouchers et on y goûte plus qu'ailleurs à York l'atmosphère d'une rue du moyenâge.

In den Shambles (*oben*), seit undenklichen Zeiten die Straße der Schlachter, spürt man die Atmosphäre einer mittelalterlichen Straße mehr als sonstwo in York. Die Straße wurde in den fünfziger Jahren sehr geschickt von der Stadtverwaltung renoviert.

We have remarked how Stonegate contains architecture of almost every age. One of the joys of the street is the building illustrated below, which clearly has a medieval origin (note the jettied upper storey) but is most noteworthy for the Victorian design in Minton tiles. It is a classic example of how, provided the scale and materials of a building are right, it can live with its neighbours in harmony, and in this case not without a sense of humour.

L'une des joies de Stonegate est le bâtiment illustré ci-dessous, visiblement d'origine médiévale (remarquez l'étage supérieur en surplomb) mais remarquable surtout pour ses carreaux de céramique décorés de l'époque victorienne.

Eine der Kostbarkeiten in Stonegate ist das oben abgebildete Gebäude, das ohne Zweifel aus dem Mittelalter stammt (man beachte das überhängende obere Stockwerk). Aber es ist vor allem bemerkenswert wegen des viktorianischen Musters in Minton-Kacheln. Es verrät einen gewissen Humor.

Bowes Morrell House (*below*) in Walmgate is a timber-framed house of the late fourteenth century, and is of great interest for its fine framing and unusual plan, which has no known parallel in the city. The roof is a fine example of the king-post type developed in York in the fourteenth and fifteenth centuries. The whole house is an excellent example of timber framing from the heyday of York's prosperous medieval times. It was restored by the York Civic Trust in 1966.

Bowes Morrell House (*ci-dessus*) dans Walmgate, de la fin du 14e siècle est très intéressante, surtout pour son fin colombage et son plan très curieux, unique dans la ville. Le plafond est typique du style à poutres renforcées développé à York aux 14e et 15e siècles. Cette maison fut restaurée en 1966 par le York Civic Trust.

Bowes Morrell House (*oben*) in Walmgate ist ein Fachwerkhaus des späten 14. Jahrhunderts. Es ist besonders interessant wegen seines schönen Fachwerks und ungewöhnlichen Grundrisses. Das Dach ist von einer besonderen, im 14. und 15. Jahrhundert in York entwickelten Konstruktion. Das Haus ist typisch für das Haus eines mittelalterlichen Kaufmanns. Es wurde 1966 durch Bürgerinitiative erneuert.

Castlegate House (*below*) is one of the best examples of the work of John Carr, and is a classic example of Georgian architecture. It was designed by Carr for Peter Johnson, Recorder of York 1759–89. Noteworthy are the shallow round-headed arches, which were a favourite device of Robert Adam, with whom John Carr had worked at Harewood House. Note the doorway, which has a pedimental-headed porch with columns.

Castlegate House (*ci-dessus*) est l'œuvre de John Carr et est un exemple classique de l'architecture du 18e siècle. Elle fut exécutée pour Peter Johnson, archiviste de York de 1759 à 1789.

Castlegate House (*oben*), ein Werk John Carrs, ist ein klassisches Beispiel für georgische Architektur. Es wurde entworfen für Peter Johnson, Stadtrichter von York 1759–1789. Gegenüber liegt Fairfax House, ebenfalls von John Carr gebaut.

The Law Courts building in Clifford Street (*below*) is the focal point in York's only wholly Victorian street. Erected in 1890, the building incorporates so many different kinds of architecture that it is probably the only building in York which displays facets of the Gothic, Byzantine, Renaissance and Victorian eras. All in all it is a most fascinating study in architecture, and the kind of building which will never be repeated. The Victorian contribution to the architecture of the city was a substantial one, now becoming more fully appreciated.

Le palais de justice dans Clifford Street (*ci-dessous*) est le centre d'intérêt de la seule rue victorienne d'York. Erigé en 1890, ce bâtiment offre un mélange de différents styles d'architecture.

Die Law Courts in Clifford Street (*oben*) sind der Mittelpunkt dieser einzigen rein viktorianischen Straße in York. Das 1890 errichtete Gebäude enthält viele verschiedene Baustile und ist faszinierend als Ausdruck seiner Zeit.

The Railway

George Hudson as Lord Mayor of York.

Bench end from Queen Victoria's coach in National Railway Museum.

It was between 1830 and 1849 that England experienced the great railway boom, and no city was more closely affected than York, largely due to the work of George Hudson (a friend of George Stephenson), who became known as 'the Railway King'. It has ever since been a major centre of English railways.

The station itself, which is one of the finest examples in existence of Victorian railway architecture, was built in 1877, at which time it was said to be the biggest in the world.

Fittingly, York is now the home of the National Railway Museum.

C'est entre 1830 et 1849 que l'Angleterre subit la grande explosion des chemins de fer et York fut la ville la plus affectée par cette explosion, du fait des travaux de George Hudson (un ami de George Stephenson) que l'on appelait « le roi des chemins de fer ».

La gare fut construite en 1877.

Zwischen 1830 und 1849 erlebte England eine Hochkonjunktur im Eisenbahnbau, und keine Stadt war mehr davon betroffen als York, vor allem wegen der Tätigkeit von George Hudson (ein Freund George Stephensons), der berühmt wurde als der „Eisenbahnkönig".

Der Bahnhof wurde 1877 gebaut.

ISBN 0-7117-0191-1
© 1989 Jarrold Colour Publications, Norwich
Printed in Great Britain. 4/89

York Railway Station.